A hole in my tooth

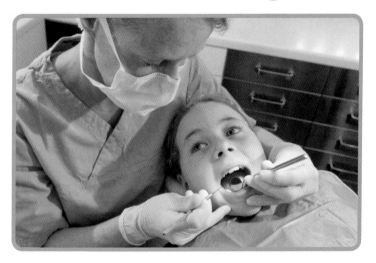

Written by Gill Munton

C000171582

Speed Sounds

Consonants   *Ask children to say the sounds.*

f	l	m	n	r	s	v	z	sh	th	ng
ff	ll	mm	nn	rr	ss	ve	zz			nk
(ph)	le	mb	kn	wr	se		se			
					ce		s			

b	c	d	g	h	j	p	qu	t	w	x	y	ch
bb	k	dd	gg		g	pp		tt	**(wh)**			tch
	ck				ge							

Each box contains one sound but sometimes more than one grapheme.
*Focus graphemes for this story are **circled**.*

Vowels

Ask children to say the sounds in and out of order.

a	e	i	o	u	ay	ee	igh	ow
	ea				a-e	ea	i-e	o-e
						y	ie	o
						e	i	
at	hen	in	on	up	day	see	high	blow

oo	oo	ar	or	air	ir	ou	oy
u-e			oor	are	ur		oi
ue			ore		er		
zoo	look	car	for	fair	whirl	shout	boy

Story Green Words

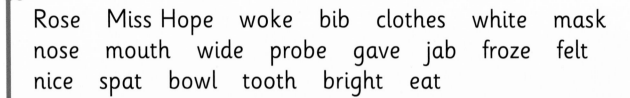

Rose   Miss Hope   woke   bib   clothes   white   mask
nose   mouth   wide   probe   gave   jab   froze   felt
nice   spat   bowl   tooth   bright   eat

Ask children to say the syllables and then read the whole word.

Mon|day   Fri|day   den|tist   plas|tic   pro|tect   in|side
met|al   de|cay   tooth|paste   mouth|wash*

Ask children to read the root first and then the whole word with the suffix.

phone → phoned   poke → poked   gum → gums
drill → drilled   fill → filling   close → closed   clean → cleaned
taste → tasted   note → notes   cake → cakes

*Challenge Word

6

Vocabulary Check

Discuss the meaning (as used in the non-fiction text) after the children have read the word.

	definition
bib	something you wear to stop your clothes getting dirty
protect	keep clean or safe
jab	an injection which makes sure there is no pain when a tooth is drilled
froze	made cold and numb
gums	the fleshy part of your mouth which holds your teeth
decay	the rotten part of a tooth that has gone bad

Red Words

Ask children to practise reading the words across the rows, down the columns and in and out of order clearly and quickly.

was	some	want	your
you	to	of	are
two	was	above	one
any	what	were	they
does	could	all	saw

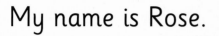

My name is Rose.

Last Monday, before I woke up, Mum phoned the dentist. I needed to go for a check-up.

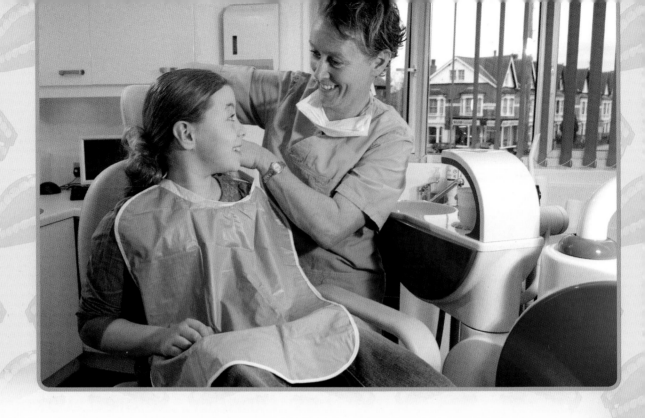

I went to the dentist on Friday.

The dentist's name was Miss Hope.

First, she put a plastic bib on me to protect my clothes.

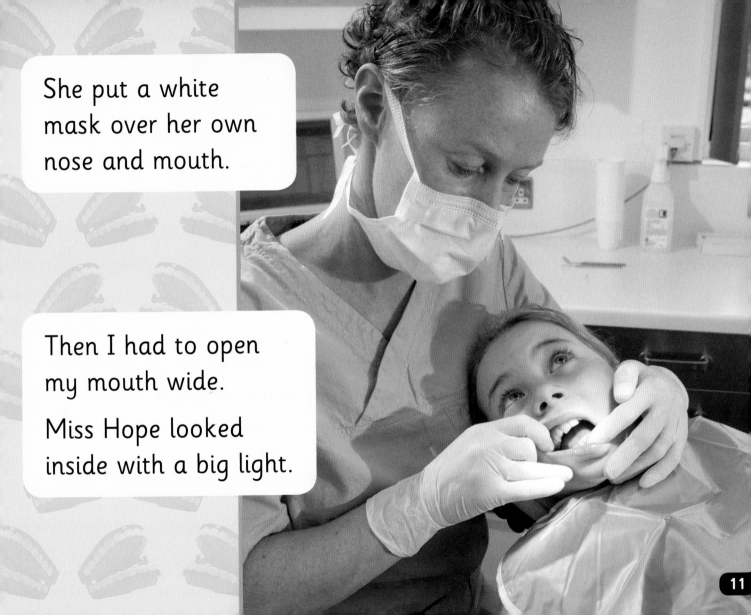

She put a white mask over her own nose and mouth.

Then I had to open my mouth wide.

Miss Hope looked inside with a big light.

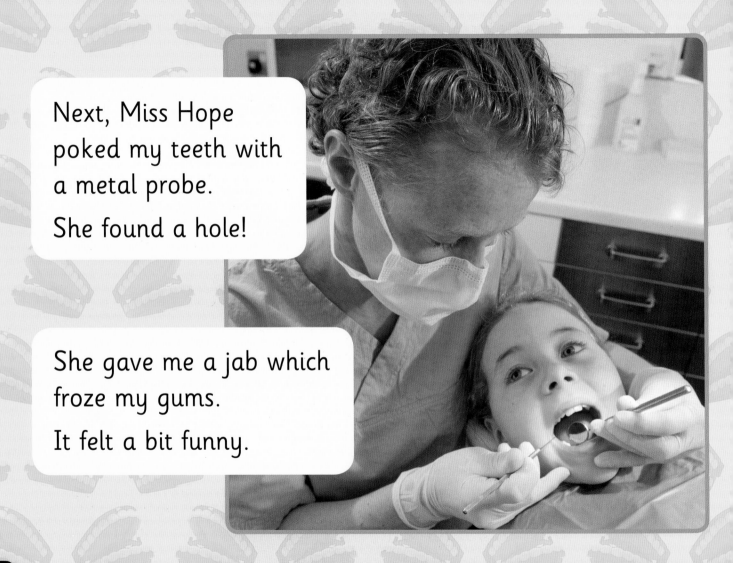

Next, Miss Hope poked my teeth with a metal probe.

She found a hole!

She gave me a jab which froze my gums.

It felt a bit funny.

Next, she drilled out some bits of decay.

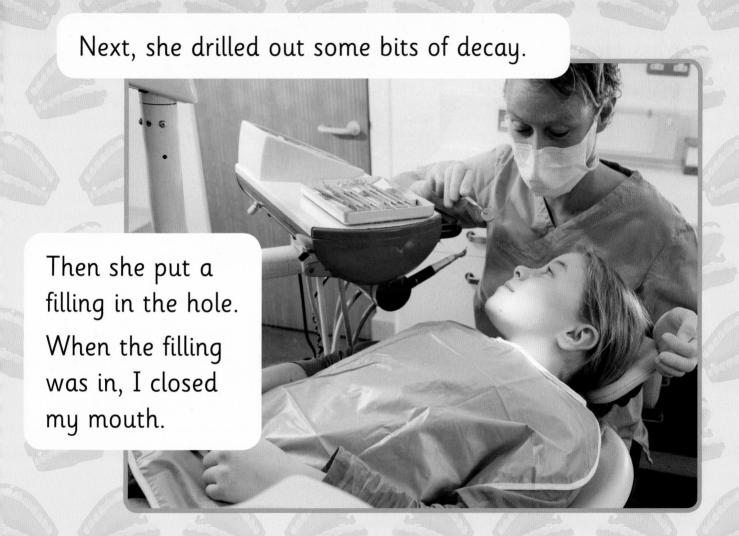

Then she put a filling in the hole.

When the filling was in, I closed my mouth.

Miss Hope cleaned my teeth with pink toothpaste.

It tasted nice.

Then I washed out my mouth with mouthwash and spat it out in a bowl.